Get the Job You Love Workbook

By Nicole Coggan

©Nicole Coggan. All Rights Reserved

ISBN 978-1-291-73079-1

A Letter From Me To You

Dear Readers,

Thank you so much for coming with me on this journey. Although I've never had a problem finding work (even if it was in a factory or shearing sheds), I do know what a struggle it can be to work out what you actually want to be do, or worse, when you get so far down a certain path and then realise it's not for you. For that reason, I've included a whole bunch of stuff related to working out what it is you want to do so this NEVER happens to you (it can be a tiny bit soul destroying). I've also included all the stuff you need to work on to actually make your work dreams a reality.

Anyway, back to how HARD it can be to work out what you want to be when you grow up (I didn't figure this out until I was 23 and still made heaps of wrong turns). When I was in primary school I really wanted to be a teacher, however, that all went out the window when I turned 13 and developed an extreme crush on this scrawny boy who lived up the road. (I decided I just wanted to marry the scrawny kid and have his babies). Thankfully, he had no interest in me so that stage didn't last!

By the time I'd finished school I was too busy being distracted by boys to bother with a career, so I just got a job at a local factory where I worked for the next 3 years. One day, I decided to move to this little country town in the middle of nowhere where I got a job in the local shearing sheds. It was about this time I realised I actually wanted to like what I was doing and have a 'career'. At the same time, the council was offering a traineeship in Automotive Servicing as a pre-empt to a Diesel Fitting Apprenticeship. For some reason, I decided I wanted to be a Diesel Fitter. I have no idea why this seemed like a good idea since I had zero interest in cars and trucks, and no mechanical ability. That said, I got the job and spent the next 12 months completing my traineeship (which I somehow managed to pass).

After 12 months, I knew the work wasn't for me but was no closer to working out what *was* the right job for me. I decided to take a 'working holiday' around Australia and try to figure this out. Amongst a whole bunch of other stuff, I tried gardening, cleaning, cooking, working in a post office, working in a bar, car detailing and washing dishes, but aside from having a great time and meeting some awesome people, I was still stumped when it came to finding a job I loved. What I did learn was how to get a job and quick. I learnt to target my resume, write kick arse cover letters, and blow employers away in interviews.

Towards the end of my trip, I landed in Darwin and it was love at first sight. I loved Darwin and decided this was going to be home for the foreseeable future. It was here that I got my first bit of inspiration. I'd landed in one of the government run employment offices because it was free to print off as many copies of my resume as I needed, and it was while waiting for the photocopier and watching the employment consultants help others with their resumes I realised I wanted to be an Employment Consultant as well.

Of course, with no formal training and no professional experience, it was going to be an uphill battle getting my foot in the door. Lucky for me I'd had all that experience with writing resumes, because I needed to create a masterpiece to get me an interview. To cut a long story short, I wrote the best skill-based resume ever, followed it up with a kick arse cover letter, and set a target of contacting at least 10 employment related services every week. I had my first interview and job within three weeks.

I loved going to work, and have been working in Employment Services ever since. Now I've taken everything I've learnt over the past eight years and put it in a workbook to help you discover your dream job and set an action plan to get results.

Can't wait to see your results!

XXOO Nic

A Glance at The Past

Okay, before you get started on mapping out your future, you first need to have a look at your past and what you learnt from it. Even if your past jobs have NOTHING to do with your future job, you will have still learnt something you can take with you. Even if that something was simply how to make sure you got to work on time!

My Job	Things I Learnt From It
Admin Officer at Bully Signs	How to format tables in MS Word, How to operate a switchboard, MYOB accounting system (Basic), that I don't like to be micromanaged

Make Sure It's Going To Be A Job You Love!

(Because trust me, there isn't anything more soul destroying than ending up in a career only to find that in reality you HATE it.)

Skimp on the following exercise at your own risk!

Do not cheat! Yep, we are always tempted to say 'yes' because we have our hearts set on something, but be honest or regret it later!

Is travel important to you? Domestic or International? Local or Interstate?

```
┌─────────────────────────────────────────────┐
│                                             │
│                                             │
│                                             │
└─────────────────────────────────────────────┘
```

Do you need flexibility to cater for small children, pets, ill relatives?

```
┌─────────────────────────────────────────────┐
│                                             │
│                                             │
│                                             │
└─────────────────────────────────────────────┘
```

How many holidays do you need every year?

```
┌─────────────────────────────────────────────┐
│                                             │
│                                             │
│                                             │
└─────────────────────────────────────────────┘
```

Is routine important to you, or do you thrive on shift work?

hat is the minimum amount of money you need to make?

What amount of money do you want to make?

Is a fly In/fly out role suitable? Can you work away from home?

How long can you work away from home for?

Do you need weekends off?

Can you work night shift?

___

Are you able to handle being on call? (Note: Usually this means you can't be over the legal drinking limit for the whole time you are on call, so if you like to get tipsy every weekend, this is probably going to make you tear your hair out.)

___

Can you start work at short notice, or do you need set hours?

___

Do you need sick leave and all the benefits that come with full time?

___

Do you like working with people?

___

Can you handle working with small children?

___

Do loud noises bug you?

Are you okay with wearing a uniform?

Are you cool with being supervised by others?

Do you need to be the boss?

Do you prefer to work alone or with a team?

Do you prefer to work with large or small teams?

Do you prefer to work indoors or outdoors?

Do you mind getting dirty?

Do you need constant stimulation, or do you prefer routine?

Are you good with numbers?

Does reading give you a headache?

Are you cool with having conditions attached to your private life? For example, in some occupations it would be considered inappropriate to be seen dancing naked on a table on a Friday night, in others no one would bat an eyelid.

Can you pass a drug or alcohol test?

```
┌─────────────────────────────────────────────┐
│                                             │
│                                             │
│                                             │
└─────────────────────────────────────────────┘
```

To really get the maximum benefit out of the above exercise, I need you to keep this in a safe place, and every time you go to apply for a job, check it against the advertisement to ensure it matches your requirements.

Who Do You Want To Work With?

Co-workers and employers can make or break your workplace happiness, so it's a good idea to work out what sort of qualities you look for in your team or boss. Obviously, this is something you can't suss out from the job advertisement, but you may be able to get a good idea about it from your interview.

I've compiled a handy checklist that you can keep in mind on the next page, but first you may want to check out a recent blog post I wrote about interview warning signs.☺

5 Interview Warning Signs it's Not The Right Job For You

Now, I realise that if you are like me, and 99.9% of the population, when you go for an interview it's all about impressing the panel to choose you over the other applicants. It's not until later (usually when you are totally miserable and wondering why you ever applied for the job in the first place), that you realise there were a whole mountain load of clues during the interview that this was not going to be the dream job you imagined it to be. So, to save all that heartache, I've compiled a list of 5 clues this is not the job for you. In no particular order these are:

The interviewer bitches about current staff members – This may occur in formats such as, "Well, the real reason I need someone is because we have this one girl, Megan, who is lazy, but we can't fire her because the government has made it so hard to sack someone these days," or in a more subtle way, such as, "You seem so much more motivated than our other staff members". Either format is bad news for you. Remember, if the boss is willing to bitch about others to someone they just met, the day will come when they do the same to you.

The interviewer tells you what a family friendly workplace it is, but you find out the manager only sees their own kids once a week because work is too busy the rest of the time – This is NOT going to be a family friendly workplace. It may have initially started out that way, but if the manager doesn't practice 'family friendly', the rest of the workplace won't either. This actually happened to a client of mine who, after the birth of her third child, really wanted to work somewhere with flexi time and other family friendly practices. At the interview, the panel nearly fell over themselves telling her what a 'family friendly' place it was to work, and although my client had heard on the grapevine that the manager was so focused on his career that he had two full time nannies, and Thursday nights were the only night he saw his children, she took the job anyway.

Three months later, she resigned. Although there was a flexi-time agreement in place, she never actually got approved to take it, and whenever she needed time off because her child was sick, she felt actively pressured to come into work anyway. If you want family friendly, ask around and do your research before committing.

Your gut instinct screams "No" – I am so guilty of this one. You read the advertisement and it looks like your dream job. You get super excited, submit your application and attend the interview. Although 'something just doesn't feel right,' you are totally pumped when you get the job. Three months later, your dream job turns into your worst nightmare, or is just not all it was cracked up to be. Basically, you let your mind override your gut and now have to suffer the consequences. In future, if something 'just doesn't feel right,' listen to your instincts.

When you interview for the job, it is at a different pay rate or conditions than advertised - Uhh, one word for this – DODGY. This is more common in certain industries than others - sales is a good example. The advertisement promises X amount of money, so you apply and get an interview (usually straight away - this is part of their 'pitch' not a regular old interview). Surprise, they tell you in the interview that you have the job. You are pumped until they add, almost as an afterthought, that your pay rate is based on commission and the advertised rate was an 'example' of how much money you *could* make.

Now, this is a little embarrassing, but years ago when I was in my teens, I actually got suckered in by this one. I was eager to get my first 'real job' so when I saw an advertisement for a 'Water Sales Person' paying $30 an hour, I was very keen. I sent out my resume and got interviewed immediately. Two minutes into the interview they offered me the job. Success, my first job after two minutes! Well, I was so grateful, I probably looked like a blubbering mess, thanking them for the opportunity. Imagine my horror when, two seconds later, they explained my wage is based on commission.

Of course, I already felt committed to the role so although I felt 'had,' I still rocked up to work anyway. I worked there for five days, selling water door to door, and pocketed about $50 for my 40 hour week. Maybe I was just a bad salesperson (that's very possible) but I noticed zero of my co-workers did any better. Don't make my mistake – if they change the ball game at the interview, they are dodgy. Leave. Immediately. (Also leave if they offer to pay you in free pizza – no shit, this has actually happened).

They want a one day (or worse, one week) trial without pay – This is illegal, but I'm amazed by how often it happens. Now, it's perfectly normal for an employer to want to trial you. It makes good business sense and I would never hire anyone without this in place. But they have to pay you for it! There was once a service station down the road from where I lived that had a different person do a one day free trial every single day. They never, ever hired anyone. Eventually, they did get caught, and besides copping a whopping fine, they got front page negative publicity in the local paper. It was no surprise they went bust not long after. Still, this didn't help the hundreds of people who had effectively donated eight hours of their day for nothing. Always ask if a trial is going to be paid, and if not, walk away. Even if they do hire you after your free week etc, it's likely they will find another way to rip you off down the track.

Now, back to your preferred qualities in an employer:

I prefer my boss to display the following qualities:

```
┌─────────────────────────────────────────────────────┐
│                                                     │
│                                                     │
│                                                     │
│                                                     │
└─────────────────────────────────────────────────────┘
```

I prefer my coworkers to display the following qualities:

```
┌─────────────────────────────────────────────────────┐
│                                                     │
│                                                     │
│                                                     │
│                                                     │
└─────────────────────────────────────────────────────┘
```

It would be really bad if my boss displayed the following behaviours:

>

I would have a hard time working with co-workers who displayed the following behaviours:

>

My Top 10

Righto, now you should have found some clarity about what a job should offer you. So, what are the top 10 things a job must offer you? In order of importance please..........

My Example:

Flexibility to take time off for my daughter's swimming carnivals

International travel opportunities

1_____

2_____

3_____

4_____

5_____

6_____

7_____

8_____

9_____

10_____

Sometimes a job won't tick all 10 of your boxes. That's why it's important to prioritise your needs. Time off for my daughter's swimming is non-negotiable, but international travel is (although I love international travel). Put a star next to anything that is non-negotiable and stick to this!

Best Day At Work... Ever

Now, time for a bit of imagination! What does your best day at work look like? Does it involve securing a new client, getting promoted, jetting off to LA to interview movie stars? Start with "When I get to work," and dream, dream, dream.

When I get to
work:_____
_____
_____
_____
_____
_____
_____
_____
_____
_____
_____
_____
_____
_____
_____
_____
_____
_____
_____
_____
_____
_____
_____
_____

101 Things You Love

Now, we've pretty much covered the conditions you need to be happy doing your job, but some of you may still be stuck on what your dream job is. To help you clarify, I want you to write down as many things as you can think of that you love doing. You can use anything that pops into your head. I'd prefer it if you came up with 101 but because that will take oodles of time, I'll settle for A LOT. For example I love:

Being creative, working alone, small teams.

My Dream Job

Describe your dream job. Put in everything that's important to you, like pay rate, how many people you work with, what sort of conditions you work in, what work you actually do. Dream big, this is not the time to think small.

What Habits Are Holding You Back From Your Dream Job?

What habits do you need to get rid of in order to move forward? These could be specific 'on the job' habits like gossiping about others, or job search related habits like procrastinating on your applications.

How to Get an Education for FREE

Is your resume lacking in the training or professional development sections? Do you need to address selection criteria that you don't actually have experience or knowledge of? It's no secret that one of the easiest ways to plump up your resume or gain experience in a subject is to get some extra education and training. The problem is often the time and cost involved. Thankfully, I've stumbled upon some awesome FREE ways to get the training you needed with flexible home study options.

So for example, let's say you are an administration officer but feel your lack of basic accounting knowledge is letting you down. You don't want to be a full blown accountant, but you believe a course in this area would provide the basic knowledge you need to get your resume out of the slush heap. Enter www.alison.com. Alison provides courses in nearly everything you can think of and it's all for free. Even better, you can work at your own pace, so if you need to submit that resume by Friday and it's already Wednesday, you can log on and hustle through the accounting basics course in time to add it to your professional development resume section in time for Friday.

I've actually used Alison myself when I've needed to learn something new for my business (like accounting fundamentals) and the course content is excellent. You do exams throughout the course, and if you pass, you can pay a small fee to have the certificate mailed out to you (or you can just print your results off online). Of course, there are some glitches because it is FREE. Alison is supported by advertising, and you are faced with annoying adverts you have to click out of for every course module. It's worth paying the little bit extra for the advertising free version. Also, it can be very slow to load.

Your other FREE option is to sign up for something like www.coursera.org which often lists free courses run by universities on various topics. Yes, you can do Harvard subjects for nothing! These courses are usually very well run, and most offer some kind of certificate on completion. Please note that most of the courses listed (including Alison) are not accredited, but you can still add them under the 'professional development' section of your resume and they get the job done as far as your knowledge is concerned.

There is a bunch of other free courses out there, but these are the two I'm personally familiar with. So next time you need an understanding of something in a hurry, or need to plump up your resume, head on over and get some of that FREE professional development training.

What Professional Development or Further Training Do You Need to Do?

Need some inspiration? Log onto www.alison.com and check out their FREE course list.

How Are You Going To Celebrate When You Get Your Dream Job?

How will you feel? What will you do? Who will you call?

When I land my dream job I will feel _____ and _____.

I will call _____, _____, _____, and _____ to tell the news.

I will celebrate by:_____
_____
_____
_____

A Note About Networking

By now you would have had to be living on another planet to not have heard about networking. Otherwise known as 'not what you know, who you know,' every Employment Consultant will mention it to you. But how do you go about it? If you're an introvert like me, asking others for help can be challenging, and it takes a lot to leave your comfort zone. Most of my employment has been found using more traditional methods, but my brother - who is probably the world's most extroverted extrovert - has got every single one of his jobs through networking, and has never once owned a resume. However, I figure you are reading this because networking is still new ground to you so to help you out, I've compiled a list:

Old Co-workers – These guys have the added value of probably already working in the industry you are interested in, and probably have loads of contacts in the industry they have met through conferences and events.

Ex-Employers – Even if they don't have a job that quite suits you available, chances are they know a whole bunch of other managers in the industry they can add in a good word for you to.

Recreational Friends – Just because the only interest you may share is a love of ice hockey, doesn't mean they don't have a cousin, aunty or best friend working in the industry. It doesn't hurt to mention that you are looking for work in the area, and do they know anyone who might be able to help (apparently we are only separated from any one person by six other people, so you could be in luck).

The Shopkeeper/Dentist/Car Mechanic – You are going to need to make small talk with these people anyway, so instead of the same old weather conversation, it won't hurt to let them know what you are looking for. For all you know, your mechanic could also service the car of the manager of the very place you want to work at.

Random Emailed Persons – By this I do not mean to randomly email every address you can get your hands on. What I do mean is express your interest in the sort of position you would like, and write a short career highlights/resume summary and send it to people on your above networking lists. Ask them if they can forward it to anyone they think may be interested in your skill set. I'd advise against this approach if your current boss doesn't know you are looking for a new job, as you have no control over where it ends up.

LinkedIn – Mmmmm, LinkedIn is huge at the moment but I'm still 50/50 on its value. If you have heaps of info you can't fit on your resume, by all means add it to your LinkedIn profile so a potential employer can see it. Other positives include the fact that you can see who your connections are also connected to, and ask for an introduction. Recruiters do often check out LinkedIn for potential candidates, I've had a number of overtures on mine, however I love what I do and I'm not ready to move on. Just don't rely on it as the be all, end all. Sign up here: www.linkedin.com

Networking Events – I'm not the biggest fan of networking events for the sake of networking events (probably because I'm an introvert and that is just too much pressure for me). I am a HUGE fan of professional development workshops, talks that involve your industry, and training courses. Not only do you learn something, but it also takes the pressure off of making connections. You can still network, but you're not forced to.

Now you know who to network with, you need to write a plan up of who you are going to approach for simple accountability. Make a checklist with the actual names, and a deadline to have it checked off by, and get to it. I'm flexible with the communication method – if the phone or in person is too much for you, private Facebook or LinkedIn messages and email will still get the job done.

Networking Contact Sheet

Name	Contact Method	Due Date	Completed
Ex: Lisa Crawly	Email	5th March	Yes

A Note About Accountability

The difference between the people who achieve their goals and the people who don't get anywhere near them usually comes down to accountability. There is no point completing this workbook if you are not going to act on the activities it contains. For example: I know the networking can be hard and you may be really tempted to skip it, but it's an important part of any job search so you need to do it. Just fill in the worksheet above, set a deadline and break it down into sections. Do five a day if it makes it easier, but do it every day until that checklist is completed.☺

You Can Do It! (And I give you full permission to eat a caramel sundae with extra marshmallows once it's completed).

Your Resume

Now I don't have room to write a whole book on resume writing for you, but I have included a tip sheet and some basic exercises you can do to make your resume better. Remember, your resume is crucial to getting you the job you love. Don't skimp on this, and if you can't or don't have time to do your resume yourself, get help or pay to have one professionally completed (at time of printing I offer a resume writing service, see back of book for details).

I've included my resume/selection criteria questionnaire that I use to pin point client achievements before writing either a resume or selection criteria for them. Not all the questions will apply to you, but fill out as many as can. Having an understanding of your achievements is vital to writing resumes, criteria, and for interview time.

PS: If you have ever read my other book 'Selection Criteria Sucks' the questions are the same.

Q. Describe a problem you recently solved at work. What was the problem? How did you solve it? What was the result?

Q. Have you completed any training, tickets or licences not listed on your resume? What were they? How could you use them in this position?

Q. Have you ever worked with cash? What amounts were you authorised for? What amounts did you handle? Did you have any added responsibility such as balancing the till, locking the money in the safe etc?

Q. Have you ever worked in customer service? What was your feedback from customers like? Did they ever give you gifts, cards or mention you in a positive light to management?

Q. Has customer services formed part of your Key Performance Indicators? What has your score been? Did you meet or exceed these targets? By how much?

Q. Have you ever participated in in house training or further professional development? For example: First Aid, Fire Warden Safety, Selling Skills?

Q. Have you had anything to do with marketing or advertising? Where were you working? What was your role? Was it successful?

Q. Have you ever made a lot of money for a business? Where were you working? How much did you make? How did you do it?

Q. Have you ever saved a lot of money for a business? Where did you work? How much did you save? How did you achieve this?

Q. Have you ever worked in a place where you had sales targets to meet? Where did you work? How did you meet them? Did you exceed them? By how much?

Q. Have you ever given a presentation or sales pitch to a crowd? Where did you work? What did you do? In front of how many people?

Q. Have you ever implemented a new way of doing things in the workplace? What was the situation? What was the result?

Q. Have you ever needed to make a hard decision? What was the decision? What was the result?

Q. Have you ever managed an investment portfolio? How much was it worth? What were your achievements?

Q. Have you ever managed a team? Where did you work? How did you manage them? How many people did you manage?

Q. Have you ever resolved a dispute? What was the situation? What was the result?

Q. Have you ever negotiated a deal with a company? What was the deal? How did this benefit the company?

Q. Have you ever had to plan a conference, party or event? For how many people? What steps did you take? What was your feedback like?

Q. Have you ever had to manage a budget? How much were you responsible for? What steps did you take to ensure you did not go over budget?

Q. Have you ever been featured in the Media? Where? What for?

Q. Have you ever written a published article? Where? What about? When?

Q. What has your feedback been like at performance reviews?

Q. Have you won any awards (Team Member of the Month etc.)

Q. What professional memberships and associations do you belong to?

Q. Have you completed any community service or volunteer work? Where? What did you do?

Q. Have you ever been rapidly promoted? Where did you work? What was the position? What was the timeframe?

Q. What computer programs do you have experience with? What do you use them for?

10 Easy Tips to Jazz up Your Job Application

1. Target your resume! It should be tailor-made for the job you are applying for. If you only follow one tip from this list, choose this one. Check out the following case study.

"Natalie had spent most of her career working in Child Protection as a Case Worker but had also worked for a number of temp agencies, doing casual hospitality and admin work when she wanted to earn some extra cash. Four months into her pregnancy, her husband received a transfer and they relocated. Natalie still wanted to work but didn't want a full time position. She was looking for a casual job with no stress, in hospitality, retail or customer service – a position where she could just do her work and go home. She sent out a very professional resume, which highlighted all her career achievements and professional history, to a number of employers. She was judged as 'overqualified' or received no response at all. She decided to change her resume. She took out all her achievements, changed the format to simple black and white and listed her temp jobs first. At the end of her resume, she listed her employment history with dates and titles – but no descriptions. It worked. She was offered a casual job in a call centre within the week."

2. Write a 'Professional Profile' section in your resume. Place it immediately after your personal details as a quick snapshot of your professional skills. Use it instead of 'Objective' in order to focus on what you will contribute, rather than what you want from the company.

For example: *"Experienced call centre operative with excellent communication skills and a passion for customer service; computer literate with the ability to operate multiple switchboards and internal programs; regularly praised by management for exceeding call handling and customer service targets".*

3. Use the correct layout on your resume. For example, if you are a recent graduate with no relevant work history, list your education and qualifications first. If you have broad work experience but lack the educational qualifications for the position you are applying for, list your professional history before your educational details.

4. Remove any character references. If you have a professional history, a list of only character references will make the employer wonder why your previous employers aren't willing to speak for you. If you don't have professional references to list, simply write 'References available on request'. If you are impressive in the interview, then you can explain why you have only character references. The only exception to this is if you are still in or have just left high school.

5. Use bullet points. When you are writing job descriptions, avoid lengthy paragraphs. Make your resume as easy to read as possible. Employers with more than 200 applications to wade through love anything easy to read.

6. Change the format on your resume. Using MS Word, go to Home, then Styles. From there you can browse and preview Headings and Subtitles until you find a style you are happy with. Choose from formal, modern, fancy and more. Hint: for resumes, less is more.

7. **Add matching borders to your resume**, cover letter and selection criteria to create a uniform appearance. You can do it easily: in MS Word go to Page Layout, then Page Borders.   Suggestion: 'Box' borders with a 3pt solid line in black.

8. **Use 11 or 12-point size font for your resume and cover letter content.** The only exception to this is if the employer is asking you to address 8 selection criteria points in a one-page cover letter. In that case, you can use 10 point to fit more in but never use anything smaller.

9. **Avoid fancy fonts (like what this book uses).** You have probably heard this one many times but standard fonts like New Times Roman are fine. Sometimes people are tempted to jazz up their resumes by using decorative fonts. Don't do it. It affects readability and doesn't look professional.

10. **Use italics and underline sparingly.** Both affect readability so use them only on titles or important pieces of information. When in doubt, bold is better.

An example of a resume using these tips, and the achievement worksheet is on the next page

DOLLY MARTIN

Address: 18 King Street, Greenland 4400

Phone: 0411 111 444

Home: 46 311 211

Email: dolly.martin@westnet.com.au

PROFESSIONAL PROFILE:

Experienced Office Manager with qualifications in Office Administration and a passion for providing superior customer service outcomes for clients; skilled in a wide range of administrative tasks with the ability to work independently or as part of a team to meet job expectations

CAREER HIGHLIGHTS:

Trusted to handle cash amounts of up to $500,000 during employment with the ANZ Bank

Consistently exceeded all Key Performance Indicators for customer service targets

Responsible for bringing in new business for O Steel through targeting a marketing flyer campaign at designated industries

Implemented all office administration procedures for the opening operations of Action

Trained new staff, prioritised jobs and assigned duties to a team of 5+ staff members during employment at Action

Winner of 'Team Member of the Month' on multiple occasions during employment at O Steel for delivering high quality solutions to customers

Competent in the use of numerous computer applications including Quickbooks, MS Office Suite, MYOB and internal programs such as Ostendo

Volunteer work within the community includes five years at the Religious Education Teacher at Kings State School and three years as a committee member for the Parents and Citizens Association of Kings State School (Including 12 months as Treasurer)

Responsible for payroll operations for 70+ staff members at TI industries

Completed Certificate IV in Office Administration through QLD TAFE in 2008 and further professional development training in MS Office Suite and MYOB

PROFESSIONAL HISTORY:

January 2013 – Current   Trade Industries

Payroll Officer

- Payroll operations for 70+ staff members on a weekly basis using Payroll software (Ostendo)
- Responsible for ensuring that all wages are allocated to the correct costings and that all allowances are paid according to company protocol
- Provide assistance to the Accountant with payment of super contributions and PAYG deductions
- Report all Payroll information to management as required and generate electronic pay slips for staff
- Create and manage employee files for new and existing staff members including salary details, commencement dates and other entitlements as specified

June 2012-December 2012   FAB Pty Ltd

Administrator

- General reception duties (both face to face and telephone)
- Provide product and service information to customers, resolve customer issues and respond to email enquiries
- Other general office and customer service duties as required

September 2008-June 2012 Action

October 2003 – September 2008 O Steel

Office Manager

- Responsible for providing quotes to customers via the phone, through email and in person
- Accounts receivable and accounts payable operations
- Resolved customer complaints and prioritised and delegated work to 5+ staff members
- Reception and switchboard operation, handling of cash payments and reconciliation

March 1993 – October 2003 ANZ Bank

Service Consultant

- Cash handling and balancing of amounts in excess of $500,000
- Handled general customer service enquiries and referrals to specialised services

REFERENCES:

Available on request

The Cover Letter

Again, I don't have room to write a whole book on cover letters (although I might get to that at some stage in the future) so I've added an easy to use template to give you the general idea on the next page.

You may notice I didn't leave a gap for the employers address and contact details. This is because so many applications are submitted electronically these days, so we no longer need to add in the employers address details. The reason I still add all your information is just to give the employer easier access should they want to call you. It saves them rifling through paperwork to find your resume and get the details from there.

You should target your cover letter for the job you are going for, however if you plan on submitting a lot of applications it's not always possible. The jury is still out on if cover letters provide that much value. Some employers swear by them and others don't even bother reading them. The thing is, you need to ALWAYS add one because even if they don't read it, they will notice that you haven't taken the time to write one.

Your Name Here

Your Street Here,

Your Town & Post Code Here

Your Phone Here

Your Email Here

Enter Date Here

Position: _____ Reference: _____

To whom it may concern,

It is with great interest I write to present my credentials for the position of _____ as advertised. I understand that you are looking for a committed and dynamic individual with a passion for _____ to work as part of your team. As a _____ with a _____ qualification and practical experience working in _____, I am certain that I have the abilities required to be a success in this position.

My current role is that of _____ for _____.
I _____ as part of my role. During this time I have achieved a number of outcomes which include _____ and _____.

I'm _____ and _____. My strong interest in _____ was developed by _____. I have also gained experience through _____. Feedback from my past employers has been _____.

Currently, I am seeking a position where I can continue to uphold strong performance and standards. Being goal oriented, I possess the energy and persistence required to succeed with both my own and _____ objectives. I would welcome the opportunity to discuss my application with you in person, and am confident that I have the experience & enthusiasm to make a significant contribution to the ongoing success and growth of _____. I appreciate your consideration and look forward to hearing from you in the near future.

Yours sincerely,

Your Name Here

The Job Search

The Three Most Common Ways To Find Employment

Advertised positions – These are positions that are advertised on either an online job search portal like Monster or Seek, or in the local newspaper. Sometimes employers will also advertise on their Facebook page, website or in their shop window. The positive of applying for an advertised position is that you can read the advertisement and get a good impression of what the job involves. It's also relatively easy to apply (usually you just fill in an online form or email through your resume and cover letter). Sadly, there is also one big negative; the amount of people who are also competing for the position. To give an example, recently the tile warehouse down the road advertised a position for a Sales Consultant to work in their showroom, and received 170 responses. That's a lot of applications to wade through and honestly, there's a good chance a lot of worthy applications would have ended up in the trash just because they were sick of looking at them.

Networking Positions – This is where you get the job or lead about the job by asking people you know if they know of anyone hiring. Sometimes you will get straight through the door without even a resume. I love this approach because even if the position is already advertised, if you are referred by somebody the employer knows, they are at least going to take the time to read your application.

Cold Calling – This is my number one favourite but most people dread it. When I went on my working holiday around Australia, 90% of my employment came through this approach. If I wanted to line up employment before I got to a town or city, I would email my resume and a cover letter explaining I was interested in temporary work to all potential employers in the area- inviting them to forward my email on to anyone they knew who might be hiring. This is what landed me a six week job filling in for an overseas staff member at a Post Office in outback Western Australia, and I received offers from a number of pubs, cattle stations and cafes across the Northern Territory.

If I had already arrived in a town or city and decided to stick around for a while, I would print my resume off at the local internet café, photocopy it and walk around handing it out at places I would like to work. This has always worked for me, and I had a bar job in Darwin within 45 minutes of starting, and two restaurant jobs at the Gold Coast just by doing the one shopping centre.

I've also used phoning the employer directly out of the phone book. This has been successful but can result in a lot of false leads and seems to have a slightly lower success rate than either email or face to face.

That said, the most effective approach for myself and clients has been an old fashioned letter in the mail with a resume attached which asks if there are any suitable positions available, and invites employers to keep the resume on file. Time and time again I have seen this work with some amazing results. For example, a recent client was looking for an administration position and had all the experience required. The issue was that she was applying for all advertised positions and the competition was crazy. She lived in a city with a low staff turnover, where you nearly had to wait for someone to die to get an employment opening, and when an opening did arrive, a ridiculously high number of suitably qualified candidates applied for it. After suggesting she try the letter approach, she wrote to 20 employers she would like to work with and put them in the post. The next week she had four interviews and two job offers.

Yes, it takes balls to put yourself out there but you can virtually wipe out 95% of the competition with this approach.

Your Job Search Plan

One word – accountability. The following excercises are designed to help you with your job search. For them to achieve this, you actually need to do ALL the excercises, not just pick and choose. When it comes to finding your dream job, this is what is going to get you there. In case you skipped the introduction, I found my dream job at 23 by setting a job search plan and sticking to it. This is your chance to do the same. Make sure you use all three methods as part of your approach.

PS: Always follow up within a week after you send in the application, call or email to ensure they received the application, and invite them to ask any questions they have. At least this way they will actually look at your resume.

How many employers are you going to contact per week?

How many of these are going to be applying for an advertised position?

How many of these are going be cold calling? (unadvertised positions)

How many people are you going to ask for leads from per week (networking)?

My Job Search Diary

Employer	Date Applied	Follow Up	Method
Billy Bunting	2nd Feb	8th Feb	Cold Call

The Interview

Ekkk, this is the part that freaks most of my clients out. I'm not going to dive into all the basics like what to wear (but ladies, check your hemline, this is not the time to go short, short). Likewise, I'm sure you already know to get there early, plan ahead for bad traffic etc.

Instead, I am going to touch on interview questions. I realise it may not seem like it, but most employers don't design their questions to trip you up. That said, I did recently see an interview question list that looked like the interviewer just wanted to look really smart and make the interviewee feel terrible. However, this is not the norm. Most employers just want to make sure you are a good fit.

Now, remember what we talked about earlier You are also interviewing them to make sure this job FITS YOUR NEEDS AS WELL. Ideally, this should be a semi-formal chat where both parties decide if it's a good fit or not, but most of the time we worry too much about what they think of us instead of the most important thing; what we think of them! After all, there's no point impressing them, getting the job, starting the job and realising that your first impression was right and this is the boss from hell!

One more warning I didn't add to 'Signs it's Not the Right Job for You'. Beware the super nice bosses. Sure, it's awesome that the boss is friendly, open and engaged in the interview, but check that they aren't 'super-duper nice' because it usually means they are overcompensating for some massive flaw that is going to make your life miserable down the track. You will know what I mean by 'super-duper nice' when you come across it. Most interviewers are friendly, that's great. But in the workplace, qualities such as fair and just are a hell of a lot more useful. Hint: If they start talking to you like you are their best friend, or want you to be, run.

Okay, now back to the questions. These days, most of the questions are going to be either knowledge based or situational based. Knowledge based is when they quiz your knowledge on something relevant to the position. *Example: "What's the difference between non-vocational and vocational barriers"?* Situational based is when they ask how you would respond in a certain situation. *Example: "A customer is very agitated about the level of service your company provided and attacks you with an axe, how do you respond?"*

Occasionally, they may also throw in one of the old chestnuts like, "What is your greatest weakness?" You have three options with this one. You can say something totally irrelevant to the job (I always say Maths because it's true and has nothing to do with resume writing). You can say something that's actually a positive for them (I'm a perfectionist; all my work has to be 100%). I find this one cheesy but I know other Employment Consultants who swear by it. Your third option is to tell the truth and hope it's not a deal breaker for them (I hate meetings because I'm always thinking about the other work I could be achieving during this time).

With regards to 'knowledge based' questions, there is little you can do to prepare but to hope it ends up being something you know the answer to. **With 'situational based' questions it's a good idea to revise the 'resume questionnaire' you have already completed and memorise some of your achievements. Where possible, always try to tie the question back to one of these achievements.** So answer the question and say, "For example, while working at X......................"

One final note is that it's always a good idea to ask questions when they ask you if you have any. Most people glide over this and say either they don't have any questions or ask something inappropriate (the interview is not the time to discuss the wage, unless they mention it). Good questions to ask are about professional development opportunities, where the business is heading or what the team is like to work with. Remember the number one thing: **You are also interviewing them to make sure the job is the right fit for you!**

Interview Impressions Job 1

Interview Impressions Job 2

Interview Impressions Job 3

Interview Impressions Job 4

Interview Impressions Job 5

Interview Impressions Job 6

Interview Impressions Job 7

Final Notes

Usually your employer will put you on a three month probation period. This is great news because you both get three months to trial if it's a good fit or not. If you discover in the first three months that it's not the job for you – please find a new job and don't stick it out because you thought it was your dream and are too frightened to admit it wasn't what you expected. You might feel that you are letting the boss down by bowing out so early, but the reality is you are doing them a favour by allowing them to find somebody who is a better fit without wasting months or years' worth of training on you.

When I was 27, I took a wrong turn and temporarily had a break from Employment Services. The contract I'd loved and worked on for so long finished and I thought that I wanted to shift my focus to Child Protection. Originally I'd started my career in employment services by working with 'at risk' homeless youths to help get them into employment, so on the surface it seemed like a good fit. In fact, I moved half way across the country for the job because I was so certain it was my dream job. I also built a five year plan around the position (involving further study and hopefully a promotion). I was so excited, but if I'm totally honest, I realised it wasn't the job for me within the first six weeks. This was a huge disappointment because I had built such dreams around it.

Ideally I should have explained to my boss that it wasn't the job for me and thanked her for the opportunity, but I didn't. The thing was, my boss was one of the best bosses I'd ever worked for and I really felt that it would let her down. Also I'd moved cross country for the job and had a five year plan. I stuck it out for another 11 months before I found the courage to make the break, but I should have done it a lot sooner. About a month after, I left I took on a training role in Employment Services and found my real passion.

Seriously guys – save everyone the heartbreak and if it's not for you, move on.

My Three Month Review

Does this job meet what I identified was important on my top 10 list?

What do I like about my job?

What don't I like about my job?

Am I happy to go to work every day?

Is there anything I could do to improve it?

Am I staying in this job for reasons that don't reflect my true potential?

Is the job everything that was promised?

What are my relationships with co-workers and the employer like?

Can I see myself still here and happy in another 12 months?

Thank you so much for coming on this journey with me. I'd love to hear your results and feedback so be sure to get in touch via email or Facebook. I can also be contacted through my website at www.nicolejessicacoggan.com.

If you enjoyed reading this book, you might want to try my other book 'Selection Criteria Sucks,' with real life examples and tips on how to write winning selection criteria. I also offer a number of online workshops and training activities via my website.

Additionally, I offer resume, cover letter and writing services, also available via the website.

XXOO

Nic

About the Author

Nicole Coggan is a passionate Employment Coach who started out helping disadvantaged youth find suitable employment opportunities before going mainstream in 2010. Her favourite thing in the whole world (besides her family) is helping others get the job of their dreams. She also hates cooking and is obsessed with Game of Thrones.

Nicole is availble for media requests, inteviews and speaking events; get in touch by email at: nic@nicolecogganresumes.com.

www.ingramcontent.com/pod-product-compliance
Lightning Source LLC
Chambersburg PA
CBHW080843170526
45158CB00009B/2615